FUCK DEATH

Mark Sargent

Fuck Death ©2024 Mark Sargent

All rights reserved. No part of this book may be reproduced, distributed, or transmitted in any form or by any means electronic or mechanical, without the prior written permission of the publisher, except in the case of brief quotations embodied in critical articles and reviews and certain other noncommercial uses permitted by copyright law.

Cover illustration by Tom Cassidy

Published by
Last Word Press
in Olympia, Washington.

ISBN: 978-1-944234-63-8
First Edition 2025
10 9 8 7 6 5 4 3 2 1

for Mirella

Contents

Emptying Pockets 1
Social Isolation 2
I'm Cool with Doom, Doc 3
Shoplifting at the One Euro Store 7
Fifty Years Ago 12
"A Cow Screams Louder Than a Carrot" 13
The Angel of the City 14
Power 16
News For the Old Crane Poet 18
Alicia's Elbow 19
We Remain Ravenous 20
Whiskey and Dog 21
Flannel Wearing Men 22
Lions Have No God 23
Elder Fool 24
Water to Rock 25
I Rupture Myself 26
Body of Work 27
The Wages of Po 30
A Taste for Neanderthal 32
Faith is the Dipstick 33
Canine Zen Master 35
I Tell Myself 36
There Are Only So Many Leaps in a Cat 38

Emergency ESP *40*

Be Fierce With Joy *41*

Water, No Less or More *42*

Lobectomy *44*

Genet *47*

Under the Radar *49*

"had the sidewalk become a breathing trampoline" *50*

Feeling Sinister *51*

The Merciless Days *53*

Hard Lessons for AES *55*

Iron Is Better *56*

Lion, or Cancer? *58*

So Much Depends Upon Celery *60*

It's Not Very Far Away But It Takes a While To Get There *61*

Nobody There *63*

Crossing Over *64*

Calamity's Child *66*

Not Flying But Falling *68*

In the Turning *70*

Something Like Summer Lurks in Laconia *71*

A Tree is Not a Woman *72*

Fuck Death *75*

Fuck Death

Emptying Pockets

I am so past too much,
it fills the rooms of my life
that become less naturally,
the value of most everything
leavened and night, night
is the setting of the sun—
I wander rooms yet to come
with a waning light in hand
whispering words as a dare
to beings a hover at the edge
of sight, they do not scare
but drift closer as if to pledge
allegiance to less, to what lasts,
I am so past too much.

Social Isolation

New to it, they write asking:
you are the Imam of isolation,
a Socrates of social distance,
pray tell, how do we live it?
I merely point out the obvious.
The first rule of social isolation is
you don't talk about social isolation.
And the second rule of social isolation...
well, you know,
ya gotta be still
for the flow to reveal
what our lives conceal.

I'm Cool with Doom, Doc

Give it to me,
the long, the short,
the sad tearful song
the management of the senses.
Are there diapers in my future?
What stages of coma
can I look forward to?
Look into?
Maybe book a bed?

Doc scratches his head
at the roots of his mane of combustibility,
a spiral of fission and its vanishing,
a derma-plumb, if you will, and
he hasn't got a fucking idea
what's wrong or, for that matter,
what's right but pulls a large rubber mallet
from his desk and says,
"This will hurt you more than it does me."
No shit, but only if I remain seated.

They keep asking my blood what's going on
but blood keeps a lid on it. Blood doesn't know
how to know what it knows. That's biology
for you, the known unknown overwhelms all
and is washed out with the tide. And then,
hours later here it comes again.

So tell me Doc, should I be shopping
for life support machines, top of the line
kit that'll keep the flow beyond the know
while humming that Motown sound?
Yeah, I second that emotion cause I
heard it through the grapevine that
I'm just about to lose my mind.
Hi de hi de, yeah.
Coo coo ka choo.
Ko ko row be sho
Diddy wah diddy
But the Doc says, Getoutaheah!
Yer clean as a thistle and just as barbed,
take your nattering and get thee gone.
No way, I say, I want another take.
Help yourself, he says, but I say
I want another opinion from you.
You're not thinking hard enough,
surely you can come up with an
obscure incurable malady that gives
mere weeks to live. Hit me with an
affliction that paralyzes, that paints
the world in lurid orange flames…
but Mirella enters the room and looks
over my shoulder and says, "Huh, you
weren't singing that song when you had it."

O who put the ram in the rama lama ding dong?
The ability to distil is valued in a mate;

especially if you believe as I do that
all memory is false and leaking and
ready to be moulded into a golden fate
in reverse, oh god we were happy!

We are all being stalked by disease,
some of them yet to be discovered,
and others have already hitched a ride
into our futures with a tick, a tease,
a riddle with no answer but to abide,
and they've made their home in your
precious abdomen and intend to hide
awhile… scalpel poised the surgeon
fought a profound compulsion to paraphrase
Ira Gershwin and how 't'aint necessarily so'
applied to all the work she did, everything
was guesswork, her doubt a bludgeon
a parasite as large as its' host, a haze
over what is seen and what is seeing,
an aimless turning of the book of days,
a relentless asking what is there to know?

I slouch out of the doctor's office, con-
demned to live, conscious on the ground
and driven to maintain this con-
versation, this internal forum, the sound
gonging, rattling the windows, push
of a word/thought, which came first?
I can't be bothered to trace the thread

back through the weave to the source.
History no longer drives my inquires,
I'm all about the surface of things now.

Going deeper complicates without revealing,
it stirs the bottom of the pond opaque,
maybe it's just all about reflection,
luxuriating in that reminder of life,
skimming across the nearly taut surface
as a six-legged creature finely articulate
and about to be eaten by a greater beast
while remaining a bundle of atomic matter.
The doctor says, That'll be twenty euros.
Come back in six months with some new material.

Shoplifting at the One Euro Store

The sun is shining but there's a snarl in the air,
I'm wearing my shoplifters' overcoat which is
not only styling but most effective for concealment
of trinkets and geegaw, baubles and bangles and
five thousand Santa figures, some with magnets,
some with strobing eyeballs and duck feet—he
can fly and swim, y'all, Santa on a ring, on a pencil,
lights in the shape of, napkins, candles, ice cube molds,
Santa swizzle sticks good god, salt and pepper shakers,
meat tenderizers, beds of nails for Barbie,
surprising number of tools, hammer and trowel,
a project comes to mind: construct something, call it
sculpture, shelter, self portrait
with the tools and the Matériel on hand
the overflowing gush of brightly hued replica
a wall to wall display that oddly, dulls
anyone over the age of five cupcake shells many sizes
suction cups on everything! Suction cups on everything
decapititated unicorn to stick on the bathroom mirror,
family living in a motel room on the edge of town
dad's disabled, mom's cleaning rooms, you're watching
your little brother while she's doing it
pliers pliers pliers and clamps on everything
that doesn't have
a suction cup
a clamp with a suction cup a clever idea comes in
many sizes many sizes from little plastic molds

irresistable chair leg pads
don't scuff up those scrubbed and buffed floors
extremely pathetic loo brushes with stands
my baby needs new knicks and they got these awful
plasticy things down here for, you got it, one euro.
One euro knicks, I'm gonna clad me wife's ass in those?
Nah. Just kidding. I got standards, damnit,
there are lines that I will not cross,
clamp with a magnet
a little tiny teddy bear with suction cup and blindfold
fifty different little cars guarranteed
to break within the hour in the hands
of anyone over say a year and a half,
those younger will just eat it,
Santa on a fucking suction cup god damn
superhero cookie cutters and stars, moons,
tarantula cookie cutters, sparkles
bags of them blizzards of falling refraction
a snow storm on Mars sparkles
bubble solution with wand,
day glow clothes pins sheets of plastic
opaque, translucent or with a rendering of
Goya's Witches Flight on a place mat a fly swatter
or fly paper, bug control for sadists, blimey,
listen to those little buggers beg for relief,
if I still had all the sets of tiny screwdrivers
in folding plastic cases I have had in fifty years
what would I have?
Pocahantas barrettes, a whole wall of barrettes,

hair pins, tiaras, scrunchies, bows, and yes, clamps,
and I'm moving slow, casual, keeping an eye
on the counter, slipping and dropping my booty
in various pockets I'm being random — hiccups of
day glo shit leaps into my hands, insists that I
conceal them and I do, I don't have the room
for loo brushes, drat, or table cloths but fistfuls
of glitter sticks fit just fine, lighters in the shape of
Godzilla and lesser lizards breathing fire
and many tiny brightly colored yet sad action figures
most too current to recognize and I slide towards the
check out with my purchases, a wire brush
and a pair of canvas work gloves for a grand
total of two euros ya gotta love it and I exit
weighted down with cheap kitsch and the useful and
no knicks, no, but I do have some one euro handcuffs.

It's the holidays, damnit, and the streets o Sparti
are busier than ever and anyone with the vaguest impulse
to beg is out there sticking out their palms like
they're checking for rain, have mercy.
Mostly its Roma and they're professionals of a sort,
not that they display much techinique,
though the colder the weather
the more likely the wee Roma waifs will be barefoot
and there's always the madonna and child motif,
it's women and girls primarily as males graduate
to hanging with the older dudes around six—
they wait till the lad insists he's bigger than that—

and a large number of them know me by sight as
the easiest mark on the street,
an old foreigner, casual, but in a hat,
dependable distributor of jingle,
the coins have a national image
while the bills are frightfully generic
the built-in mediocracy of the EU,
one of my regulars,
a beautiful five year old girl
bounces up and I reach in my pocket
grab the first thing and drop in her
waiting hand a package of table cloth weights,
that's right, with clamps attached,
"Merry fucking Christmas ya little brat."
She freezes a moment looking at her prezzie,
dumbfounded with joy she looks up and says,
"Teen aftoh, gahmoto?"
(What the fuck is this?)
I'm already roaring with laugher,
"Wear 'em as earings, girl."
I mime this, they got clamps ya know,
she gives me the 'you're fucking crazy' look
and turns away muttering.
It's great, you can't insult a Roma kid
because they don't give a shit what you think.
The next kid's lucky and gets a Godzilla lighter,
but the next few get wonder woman barrettes
including a four year old boy who throws it at me,
I'm handing out shit with a magnet

crap with a clamp
suction cupped skata,
they don't have time to refuse
the sidewalks of main street Sparti are expansive,
boulevards, y'all, with all manner of traffic and commerce,
and I'm sliding through the crowds and I turn,
in my wake are a dozen Roma comparing
each other's weird plastic crap but I'm on
to one of the lone Greek beggars
a bent dog-eared slip of a guy
ten years ago when he first appeared
I used to think, what's the story, he looks
capable of work but now, damn,
he sits on a square of cardboard
sometimes he can't raise up the used
ice cream cup to catch the change
a sad decline to be sure and I reach in
and pull out a sponge in the shape of Bambi
and lay it on him.
It doesn't appear to register,
the object in hand
it's, it's, what the fuck is it?
He sits, a comatose Diogenes staring
at a Bambi sponge and remains,
fastened to the pavement
anchoring the universe
as I turn the corner
with my pockets empty
and my head just
full of it.

Fifty Years Ago

Drifting on the Puget Sound, sails
barely full, cold cans of Oly, 16 oz
and a live Saturday matinee broadcast
of the Metropolitan Opera murmuring
from a radio in the cabin. Beverly Sills
is jabbering away during the long
intermission, approving of some
soprano's technique and a seal
pops its head out of the glassy water
and watches us drift past,
the epitome of white privilege,
though that wasn't printed on our
sweatshirts, no, the name of the boat was.
My father scans the bay in search
of a patch of wind, wanting always to go
faster. I thought this was fast enough
and awaited the third act. It was Puccini,
after all.

"A Cow Screams Louder Than a Carrot"

Said the wise man, no matter how hard you squeeze.
I've never squeezed a cow, coaxed a squirt from a teat
as a child, school outing to the dairy, get some shit on
your shoes, but no real sense of what the fuck moo is.
There was no context such as: You know, when a baby
sucks on her mum? It's the same stuff, more or less.
These cows have had babies but aren't allowed to nurse 'em.
Didn't tell us that either.

I held a carrot up to my ear and squeezed. Nothing,
doesn't even give the satisfaction of pressure applied,
a bit of yield, surrender to the grip, no,
how the carrot suffers remains with it.
But the wise man was talking the pain of killing.

I once knew a guy who worked at a slaughterhouse
and the electric zapper that fried each cow's brain
in turn gave it up and he was compelled to straddle
the chute and crush each bovine skull with a large
sledgehammer as they passed beneath.
Said if you didn't hit them just right you had to swing
again, that they staggered forth for step or two
before collapsing into the dust.
He didn't mention screams. Perhaps the blow
paralyzed the beast, broken from its slavery
and bound for our still chewing mouths?
You either do or you don't, there is no middle path.

The Angel of the City

Off a villa stuffed with art,
on a terrace above the water
stands a horse and rider.

His arms thrust crucifix wide
he leans back on the horse
head thrown ecstatic to sky,
open to whatever may come,
fingers curled, phallus at attention,
pointing across the Grand Canal.

Once upon time it could be
removed by unscrewing but
it is firmly attached now and

a young man runs his hands
over it—dense cold bronze horse
and man—describing what he feels.
A young woman watches, listens.

He looks not at the forged metal,
not at the girl, but away at how
his mind moulds the flexible matter
of the imagination from the messages
his hands deliver as they caress
the damp bronze flesh.

He murmurs in Spanish, she lingers
close by ready to lead him away,
a blindman in Venice bringing
his fingers to the art, the horse,
the angel of the city taking it all in.

Power

Who rode and were ridden across the psychedelic night bucking
and turning towards the numinous promise of morning only to
find the sun as disinterested as ever

And many comrades bemoan the ice and snow and downing
of power while here they cut off the juice regularly for fucking
hours but the temp in downtown Sparti is in the low seventies,
if yr of a Fahrenheit persuasion.

It's about the simplicity of the grid but back when labor still had
some fight they'd strike with rolling blackouts and you knew you
were six to two while down the valley they couldn't start lunch till two
And once on a plane a young man returning from private contract
work in Baghdad boasted to an old woman, who asked how it was
going, that them poor Baghdadians now had power for eight hours
a day, thanks to American know-how. The crone nodded timidly
but I could see through her thin hair and skull to the brain that was
asking: Didn't they have power 24-7 before shock and awe?

The power company keeps driving out to examine our crib's
meters, astonished at how much power we're pumping into the
system, gratis, we ain't even charging them muthafuckas and,
damnit, they just cut us off again, unannounced.

While south of here high in the mountains an English-Greek yoga
woman's bitch has given birth and one of those pups is bound to
be my bitch. I've been waiting for her since the disappearance of

the mighty Dude who was too much beast for this simple village. Usually they have shown up more promptly than this and I was tiring of waiting but the call has come. We don't know how much life we have left, of course, but I didn't want to spend any more of mine without a dog, the having of a different kind of power, moments of entry into the canine mind, and the wild.

News For the Old Crane Poet
for Dan

Morning tea amidst a sprawling orange trumpet vine
a hum with laboring bees—it looks like hard work,
landing on a blossom, crawling up the translucent petals,
rubbing against pistil and stamen and, pollen laden,
staggering back out, flying to the next blossom, repeat.

A bright yellow butterfly flits erratically by,
a lone cicada starts clacking.
The collective labor of bees and ants
is missing in much of the insect kingdom
where a pre-anarchic singularity reigns,
a mating, birthing, dying cycle perfect
in meaning, purpose and use of energy,
where everything is an enemy.

A bee lifts, heavily, off
and buzzes away in the hallucinogenic green,
hive bound perhaps,
to deliver its burden and maintain
the persistence of bee
and the triumph of the many.

Alicia's Elbow

It is not inspiration that drives the word
but curiosity that pushes the line,
the triggered memory, the overheard

goof or prank, the spring-filled bird
in the jasmine trilling song sublime,
it is not inspiration that drives the word

but air and blood, a half-note slurred
across the bridge in double time
the triggered memory, the overheard.

Instinct, hormone, a folly absurd
catches logic out, changes paradigm
it is not inspiration that drives the word

just a stumble, the clear idea deferred
the shard of glass in gravel shine,
the triggered memory, the overheard.

She dances, shouts, an archetype hotspur
banging language against the moon's rhyme,
it is not inspiration that drives the word
but the triggered memory, the overheard.

We Remain Ravenous

I steal the poem from the mouth of better days
and illegally parked, tourniquet the fabric air
into pretzel saviors whispering special memories
in the anuses of the tall and barely standing,
bent, as they are, in a most peculiar way
over engines from the future.
Wait a minute, did someone just declare: Flame on!
Or is my childhood bleeding into my dotage?
Is bleeding dotage a childhood? What are
the options: dancing or dead or done?
This dead thing is slipping into me verse
with redundant frequency, like I just discovered
it. Boomer vanity has dominated economies
yet contributed bugger all save 'more'.
And now we want more, again.
Give us another decade, damnit!
20 percent more than our grandparents
is not an unreasonable request.
We haven't eaten up all the resources yet,
there's still time to consume more.
Bring it fucking on.
We remain, ravenous,
ready to eat the face off pleasure.

Whiskey and Dog

"You smell of dog," sniffs Mirella.
Is it just me cardy?
I am reminded of a letter to the
editor in the Daily Telegraph
wherein a man declared with
some conviction that a gentleman
smelled of whiskey and dog
and never wore green wellies.
I admit, me wellies are green.

Flannel Wearing Men

Clutching coupons flannel wearing men advance.
Someone says the coupons have expired
someone says they never had any value,
that scrunching them in hand, that crinkling
paper sound is all they have to offer
and they can not be redeemed for wives.

Maybe the music of the spheres is just the wind
howling over the freshly snowed mountains,
singing the oak, olive, rattling everything?
That low moan is its alone—a man on a horse
has taken shelter in the lee of the barn he scratches
his mare behind the ear he dawns in the mind of the beast
a sugar cube a dream saddle woven from the poetry of
debunked holy men, a stream of empty promises
bubbling over the undeniable truth that not all plaid
shirts are flannel, but all men in them are mortal
and they will die in the burg they were born in.

Lions Have No God

She felt as empty as an atheist in a village church in Yorkshire on a Tuesday afternoon in February, but this was Donegal and the day far too long. Fatigued bands of grey masqueraded as light, shadows upon shadows, dark stark corners where nothing happened, her interior world had taken a gothic turn and she half-expected a man in a cape to materialize before her. Or a faith-failed cleric. Out the window a line of vegetation marked a small river crossing the landscape. Hedgerows and stone walls made a crude geometry of the rolling green hills, white puffs of black faced sheep were strewn across the fields. She shuffled through the day's mail. A postcard from Puerto Rico came to hand and she turned it over for the message.

> **I imagined robustly fucking you in the ass to roared encouragement. Or was I merely remembering? Love, Louis**

She smiled, nodded, almost laughed aloud. But really, she had never 'roared', the odd shout, a scream, perhaps. It's something men fancied themselves doing, lions bragging across the savannah in the African night, that sort of thing. Memory and fantasy have adjoining rooms and are often intimate, they seed each other. Fantasy fingers memory for an image, a setting, a narrative fragment from which to manufacture a story, a daydream of satisfaction, a tale of what might have been. A crow spreads his wings in descent and alights upon a fence post. Poor Louis, ten years dead and still remembering, still desiring, a roar from long ago and no lion to respond.

Elder Fool

Morning IPAs beneath the Lakonian sun
we drank to the end of winter
that wafted through the groves, near done
and to the success of our friend, the brewer,
who complained of making no dough.
And yet was on his feet, undismayed,
victory by nearly any name, you know,
the lads in the brewhouse are getting paid.

'You have eased into the role of elder fool,'
my son puts a jolly spin on life,
and yes, I haven't yet begun to drool
or lean too heavily on my wife;
momentum is a powerful thing,
especially when it has that swing.

Water to Rock

As a young poet I took dictation
from the language stream,
confident of voice, vain of connection,
willing to settle for the redeemed
fragments adrift in the flood,
rumored to come from the blood.
Now I re-dream every word
turning over sound and meaning
to see its texture as stone—
something of earth, hard cosmos
you can stand upon, that can break
apart beneath the proper tools.
It is a different way of using time,
a wall made without utility, a rhyme.

I Rupture Myself

I rupture myself laughing, melting out of the chair
till my face rests on the cool tile floor.
I have forgotten how handcuffs feel.
Gaia the dog comes to lick my face.
Fortuna rubs against my ear in all her calico glory.
My derelict consciousness is no match for the hard
edges of the world, the animals all realize this.
They seek to soften my stumble, cushion my careen, and fail.
A knock on the door, a shout in the dark, heralds a strain of
pretend contamination, a bovid plague.
Sweet Jaysus, hollow horned ruminants are marching upon us;
chewing and belching and dropping huge loads!
I attempt to mount but they're having none of it.
I attempt to mount but they're having none of it
and am trampled beneath their hooves,
just another particle of dust and shit,
another stick figure broken into letters.

Body of Work

The question was:
Do you have a body of work?
And sure, that rocked me back on me heels.
Body?
Ear? Thighbone? Nutsack?
A nutsack of work, a testicle bag o po
which can be swung like a dead cat
in a midnight graveyard, incantations
to dark deities groaned to the moon?

To give material form to the abstract?
He bodied forth the chutzpah of a leopard
a week from its last meal.

Well puckered the asshole of his verse,
his sonnets on their knees pleaded
for a mercy, relief for his kidneys,
his large intestines, the fucking plumbing
ain't humming, is in need of a villanelle
and a bit of terza rima, or maybe a lot?
Yeehaw, penetrate me Jesus, make me
weep and moan, there's more haiku
in me little finger than worms in the
compost, ticks on a dog, buzzes in
the bee; O be relentless, son of god,
rip me a new one into next week.

But never mind the wannabe deities
with their agents claiming the wee wafer
is the body is the body is the body,
and when you're a child you think
can the host bleed? 'Can the host bleed,'
the shite we have to shed just be awake
for a few moments till the fog rolls in.

As Mr. Creeley wrote: The plan
is the body The plan is the body.
He went on, you get the picture,
which doesn't answer the question:
the body of work, who has it and
do you? Can it stand up to the weather
and the years? What's it made of?
What's it made of? And whatever that is
can be reduced to an infinitesimal microscopic
blip of data that takes up no space at all.
Even if it can be sent a billion times
around world, into every phone on
every screen, projected on to clouds,
we know there is no body, no matter
that occupies space, that has a density,
that can loom above or cast a shadow.

No, the poet has a body but what she does
will not stop a bullet unless she's been busy,
lived long and had a collected published.
Hard copy, comrades, a brickish tome,

something for the barricades, not only to
stop the aforementioned but as a weapon
when the conflict comes down to hand to hand,
text to head, stab them with your pens, poets!

So maybe if all the poetry I've written was
collected and slapped between covers…
it wouldn't save your life, or hurt your back,
might possibly amuse, briefly,
while I will continue to slide towards the exit,
burdened by a body but fully unemployed
and scratching at the surface of things.

The Wages of Po

O the hundreds, it can't be
thousands, can it? Are there
so many? Strewn along my path
are manila folders in dented
filing cabinets smeared
with carbon copies,
carbon copies for fucks sake
are bobbing in my wake
eaten by bugs in storage spaces
in places like Tacoma.
The long paper roll
of endless daily spew
the cat shit on, it's there.
O the forests downed!

And floppy disks that
no machine can read,
let alone a poetry pilgrim.
Only the doing mattered,
just make the thing, the poem,
and move on.

They will never be revived,
though maybe, when senility
or dementia descend,
I'll be moved to rewrite them?
That has a certain Audenesque appeal.

Zen no-mind editing would seem
to favor a paring down,
reduced perhaps to noun and verb
beating against the linear conceit,
chewing the song down to
bark, snarl, kiss, lick
bone weed wing bird
breakfast
lunch
dinner
eat

A Taste for Neanderthal

No one knows when the rain will fall,
but all is gambled that it will;
hyenas had a taste for Neanderthal.

It's not likely you will turn into a ball,
become a note in a stream of jazz, still,
no one knows when the rain will fall.

Caesar marched his army into Gaul,
those who did not kneel they'd kill,
hyenas had a taste for Neanderthal.

He was robbing Peter to pay Paul
it made more sense than poison pill,
no one knows when the rain will fall.

Rhyme was a claw he used to maul
those insisting he should chill,
hyenas had a taste for Neanderthal.

Save those of Africa pure we all
have some of them in our veins still,
no one knows when the rain will fall,
hyenas had a taste for Neanderthal.

Faith is the Dipstick

I have on the mantle two ceramic polyhedrons from Ancient Greece.
They're loom weights with a hole at the apex
to hold the bundles of warp threads taut.
I've seen the same in museums dated to the 6th century B.C.

I found them after a heavy rain years and dogs past
I remember having a third but gave it away long ago,
the edge of memory splits and frays into
an instrument suitable for the lashing of buttocks.

This morning Mirella said, It's Monday the 13th
and we cried out in unison, Oh nooooo!
as though we'd discovered of a sudden that we were
in an asteroid path and found the prospect
an hilarious lark requiring melodramatic wails.

We have reached the endgame for ourselves and species
and rummage about for those fake noses
and magical cloaks woven on ancient looms.

"Life is a comedy for those who think
but a tragedy for those who feel."

Faith is the dipstick too short to reach the oil.
No matter how many times you stick it in
you have nothing to show for it

and no idea re the level of lubricant.
The whole vehicle might grind to a halt
worn down by the friction of moving parts
and left to form an iron oxide crust,
a burnt orange, a breakdown and a growth.

Canine Zen Master

Plane trees choked by ivy tower
over the shimmering snake of
noisy water rustling over rock,
through the shadows racing
towards the sea. The serpent ripples.
A leaf bobs and spins 'round
and over rock, submerged
and up again, at play in the
rush of water and air
shredded sunlight flares off
bubble and stone and of course,
I am the river, bubble and stone,
never same and constant gurgle
always going going and staying.

From behind and out of sight
Tremoula gives my ear a big lick
and instantly I am what I am,
an old man on a rock by the river.

I Tell Myself

Atop a tall ladder in an olive tree
the sense I'm about to fall is strong,
a tightened sphincter helps not at all.
I tell myself: This is the last year you gather olives.
Am I premature in this declaration?
Do I tempt fate?
Fuck fate, I don't have the mojo to keep doing what I did
20, 30 years ago,
nor the motivation,
and good riddance to that.
I tell myself: get through this year
and then someone else can do it.

But who would that be?

There are city dwellers who claim,
without a shred of evidence, that
the crisis has inspired young Greeks
to return to the land.
This is romantic nonsense.
There is a labor shortage in Lakonia.
Growers walk into cafes full of able bodied
citizens asking if anyone wants to work,
50 euros a day and lunch. No takers.

Young Greeks have no interest in farm work
and who can blame them.

The money is shit, the work is hard,
you're at the mercy of the elements
and you might hurt yourself:
cut off a finger, hurt your back,
fall off a ladder.
Rich river bottom land lies fallow.
Evermore mechanization and labor from afar,
men who have suffered to get here,
brings in the olives.

I tell myself: shut up,
listen to the birds,
pick the olives,
write the damn poem.

There Are Only So Many Leaps in a Cat

Paw pierced and tangled she cried
her most human lamentation:
tuned to the mammal in us
forever vigilant for dependent young
that wail arrives through
the skin as well as by sonic vibration.
We rise from our seats to see.
Seized within twists of thorny bougainvillea
Fortuna cried like the infant she is. We talk
reassuringly, "Breathe, kitty, I can do this.
Jesus fuck, how did you do that?"
On stomach I reach through wrought iron
and dense thorny vine to her predicament,
place one hand beneath her for comfort and
with the other push the punishing vines apart.
Released she sprints away to the others.
They get caught in human contraption
or by creatures larger and ill tempered.
If you live with them
you'll get a chance to save
their lives, that's how it works.
Emily meanders about the house,
ancient, deaf, smashed ear, broken tail,
the wounds of a wild life, and senile.
Saved her from strangulation once, now she
can't remember that she pisses outdoors
and squats over a salad bowl instead.

Even my mother didn't do that.
So if there is a judgment day
I hope the jury is made up
of different species. Makes sense,
well, as much as any afterlife scenario.
If they seat cats I'm sure to be acquitted,
allowed entrance, given a cushion to sit on.
But what if my mother's on that jury?
I'm prepared for that.
"It got a laugh, mom."
"It did? Well, okay then.
Nothing is harder than comedy."

Emergency ESP

Tiny Tit bounces 'bout the bougainvillea branches,
pauses to peruse the food below in cat dish.
Frieda, one of the wee sisters, as still as stone
coils in focused crouch, pounce triggered.
Through the window I clench my brain beaming
one message only: chill, bird, don't do it.
Tit bobs and hops, tweets and peeps,
does a sideways shuffle and flits off.
Whew. You feed the cat and save the bird,
the contradictions are exhausting.
Far closer to the end than the beginning
I find my joy through care of the living.

Be Fierce With Joy

Be fierce with joy, I tell the dog,
she nods, but acts as though she
hasn't a clue, even less than that.
After the fact, joy doesn't know
itself, is a matter of interpretation
and Gaia don't interpret no how.

She's straight sensualist, sound goes
in one ear and stays there, she sees
the same and tastes only barely,
gobbling with hungry haste but smell,
what floats in the air, what comes to
her raised snout, is beyond savor:

twitches of olfactory phantom forms
balleting, invisible, smashed idol tears
shivering and sliding down the face of
the world — there is a crow and an owl
and a boar colluding, there is the urine
of a dozen donkeys past their due date,

five of them have stood in a fig orchard
three days hence and one of them is preg
nant. She cannot share this data, this
atmospheric map and I kneel before her
talking: granola, tangerine, Chinese green
tea, Kilchoman, Leffe, hortopita, Mirella.

Water, No Less or More

Is there less water in the world?
Or is it impossible for it to escape
and so the same amount as ever?
There's no where for it to go.
So it's not supply but demand.

Something about tasting the animal,
the living thing of the river—
as though drinking is making less
which isn't, just moving around,
seeking the shape and filling it all,
water can measure the size of anything.
Where hasn't it been?

A map perhaps is in order, veins as a sense
of flow, defeat of the static, motion sans meaning
save gravity, without which water is nonsense.
Nothing works without planet suck.

So be kind to water. Drink much and carry it
away to somewhere else and piss it out, try it off
balconies often, lawns and bushes, and the compost
awaits your offering, a nitrogen enhancing arc,
if you're male and aiming, but however, from a squat
or with leg raised, make your offering.
It steams on a cold day and disappears into earth
on a hot one and oh how the ocean loves it,

a circuit completed, an equilibrium attained,
water come to water but does not make more,
for the flux cannot be measured.

Lobectomy

BEGINNING SPRING IN THE LOCKED DOWN MOUNTAIN-LESS CITY I LEAN ON MIRELLA AND STAGGER AFTER THE LEAPING FORWARD SUN

(*Note: While I have no symptoms, the pictures reveal a wee tumor which necessitates the removal of the upper lobe of my left lung. Success, they claim, the patient will live to endure further as yet to be determined trials.*)

1.
THICK, DARK & HAIRY HE ARRIVES BEAMING:
"I will say no to nothing!"
He's a bear with a beehive,
wading in a salmon swollen river
eating and drinking everything in reach
with both paws—what appetite
what thirst! And he has become
the go-to guy for gay reality
as staged by German TV
on the island of Crete.
He does not fall down.
When I need blood
he offers his arm.
He is a bear and has much to share.

2.
GREEK INDEPENDENCE DAY 2021
Lovers of air

doves soar about the hospital
mocking the vanity of the ill
with constant calls of you, you, you.
Awakened from the pursuits of night
by nurses' need to measure
bedridden eyes go with them
as they drape the dawn
with ribbons of flight.

3.

DESCENT INTO DAY
...a cloud of monkeys blows through the trees
introducing a stormy melody ...at lips a horn
but no notes are played ...light flash off brass
...stone hurled into the mosaic mirror
the gears of dawn crank up the blue dome.
When I cough my lessened lung
tries to escape my chest while muscle
and bone struggle to hold it fast.
Out the window a city of five million lies,
exhausted, broken by the lords of finance,
shut down by the invisible mystery of virus.
Everywhere the paint is peeling,
the pavement buckled, lights burnt out,
Athína's a fifty cent peep show
in an age of glossy free pornography.
Fatigued by ache, I ease back
from the metropolis into pillow,
pull up blanket, cup balls with right hand.
Wobbly, attempting to roll,

I feel like an early discarded prototype
in the invention of the wheel.

4.

EASY

Down past the nurses' station
in shabby pajama pants, pilly cardy,
plastic toilet seat cover in one pocket,
baby wipes in the other,
my ruse is working until the arrival
of my elegantly dressed wife.
It's easy to be seventy—
you're way past the hump, which,
to be vague, is that twenty between
forty and sixty—
children grown, parents dead,
the garden is rich with years
of compost, manure and worm,
take any seed that's thrown.
Helps if your partner is still on the hump.
Mass murderer in the corridor of the hospital
cackles across the linoleum as though
he'd just invented Korean ghost movies.
I know better and hold my tongue
between forefinger and thumb.
Death takes the elevator up to floors
without number. I take the stairs,
one step at a time, back to the earth.

Genet

I look like Genet.
That's what I think
looking in the mirror.
After summoning a pic
of St. Jean, nah, it's just
the penal sheering,
the boot camp burr.
My head is rounder,
there's no suspicion or anger,
my suffering in a minor key.

Genet was imprisoned
for lewd acts among other
petty crimes such as
vagabondage and
selling his ass and mouth.
Vagabondage, they used to
call it vagrancy in the States,
too casual for Kansas,
out of touch in Okanogan,
lurking with no place to flop.
If the heat didn't like your look,
(hair many inches longer then)
they'd threaten you with it:
There's no place for you here, boy,
I suggest you keep on moving.

Now you can crash anywhere
and they'll give ya tent and a bag.
Shit, we had to steal that stuff
back when we were neglecting
to have permanent addresses
and sleeping under the rhododendrons.

We can be sure Genet slept rough
many nights sans tente ni sac de couchage.
Que diable!

My hair will grow
my head may sort itself out
I will never learn French
and hundreds of sunrises
brilliant and dull, vivid tears
along the Parnona ridge
to a symphony of birds
are relentlessly enroute,
with or without me.
Whew, what a relief.

Under the Radar

It is so very nice to remain
under the radar, off the grid
if not the map, non grata persona
without introduction, let alone invite;
but the dogs give not a shit for fame,
the seminar, the fellowship,
and though oft in repose, have shown a
a gift for devotion, whatever I write.

By the credential of my scent,
they are sure of who I am
and always know which way they went,
whether poet, boar or wee lost lamb.

Privilege to care for the tribe of canine;
I am theirs, and they are mine.

"had the sidewalk become a breathing trampoline"

For d & C

Were things torn along the bias just to satisfy the gods who were pretending to exist on popcorn and aspirin? They lurked about in the projection room performing emergency splices, they called them, which were nothing more than eyes-closed life chop: from Topeka to Tripoli in a blink, a living montage of unfulfilled gesture torqued. And torn again, this time by an unrevealed genius wearing a button that read: I TOO TURTLE. The sticky farts that linger, the reverse mayonnaise promising lubrication and continuous blackout, total insect domination by tangerine spiders, as birds are from fish, eight eyes polarizing the zing to navigate without antenna, without charts or hoodlums. Just airborne with each exhalation, floating for a moment before descending to tender concrete flexing like a lung. Boing. Boing. Dogs running in their dreams. Scoom.

Feeling Sinister

Having taken out a lease on a shriek
but intent on holding it in reserve
I stepped out into the street feeling sinister.

Enemies made of sewer steam lounged
leaning against decaying brick walls
with their sardine fingers and arcane
interpretations of empire and faith.

Fish mouths chewed the texture of grit
and brick, the baked clay earth chalk
carried along what can hardly be called
a tongue in the sense of a love muscle.

And yet, though I quite like to entertain
the idea of sinister, I end up causing this
mental query in the minds of the old fucks
at a nearby café: Who is the guy in the
porkpie handing out chickens to Roma
women outside the supermarket?

Who indeed? Guilty. There is, perhaps,
a place reserved in Roma heaven for me,
though I can't imagine what it looks like.
There'd be music, you'd think, and what?
The ones round here are Christian, sort of,
but that doesn't help as I don't have a grip

on Christian heaven besides the cartoon version,
you know, people walking on clouds and
wondering how the others ever got in.

And I'm not sure the wings will fit cause
while I'm buying the rather expensive
organic chicken for my crib, I'm copping
the cheap agra-biz birds for my gypsy gals.
They don't care. Life will grind them down
long before the evils of commercial chicken.

It's not a balance we strike, no, nothing as grand
as that; rather, they provide me with a chance
to think I'm not a complete bastard (sinister)
hoarding my more than ample resources just
because I can't let go. Such a deal,
for a few cheap birds I stroll the Spartan boulevards
with a modicum of equanimity, unhindered by
the march of history and the stain of the bourgeoise.

Note to kindred spirits. When considering your
position in society, and the responsibilities thereof,
relax, take it easy, don't drive a hard bargain for
in the end none of it will save anyone, ever.
We weren't granted that power, whew.

The Merciless Days

O merde, o mercy,
a wee kitten with its hind legs crushed
crawls towards the curb.
We drivers take care to avoid her,
granting a few more agonizing moments.
Out of the way she writhes,
mouth stretched in a silent cry
that vanishes in the afternoon heat.
Up the serpentine road towards the village
near every car waves or flashes their lights.
What are they saying?
'The village is on fire! Turn around!'?
But there's no smoke above and I can
only conclude those signalling are saying
'You're good, Mark, keep doing
whatever it is you do.'
That ain't it either, though it's true,
they don't know what I do,
have never read a word I've written,
and wouldn't, even if it was in Greek.
In other words, I'm free,
and they sense that and approve.
That's the way I look at it.
Earlier in the day I suddenly heard
a Hurdy Gurdy coming my way
and cranked by a woman.
I jam my hands in my pockets,

drat, no change. I open my wallet,
damn, the smallest bill is a tenner,
but honor must be served and the
Hurdy Gurdy woman must be paid.
She's not singing songs of love
but she's grinding it out real good.
Is the level of pain in the world constant?
Or does it rise and fall with the moon
or other phenomena out of our control?
I fear it will it always overwhelm joy,
that's just the charge the living carry---
the current flows, the electricity jumps,
everything is illuminated and fades,
leaving pain and our efforts to avoid it.

Hard Lessons for AES

Children must be schooled in subterfuge
they must be taught to skim the surface
as tranquilly as possible, improvising on
expectation, anticipating others' obedience.
No one can talk the issue out, cunning
is acquired like learning tennis, nobody
picks up a racket and thumps it like Serena,
it takes practice to fool some of the people
most of the time, which is pretty much
all you can hope for; like everything else
there is prescribed path and there is the
shortest route to what is desired.
Fair is for games when the outcome
is secondary to participation whereas
trickery, misdirection and connivance
are for when victory is of the essence.
Elections, revolutions are not won by
adherence to law, rather they are driven
by what transcends the habits of history:
truth is fluid, the reins of power temporary.
The tortoise is slow and sure,
the hare is fast and distracted,
but when they arrive for the prize
coyote has already won with lies.

Iron Is Better

He had me going till
the envy gremlin reared
its pointy purple head
and sought to compare
ills and misfortune,
as though the playing field
is level and everyone has
the same kit, same gifts
or lack of, same leverage
on the tilt of planet,
which amounts to squat,
less than, if yr keeping score.
The explanation is always this
is not that, yeah, iron is better
than marshmallow, Irish reels
are better than mustard, I like
oatmeal cookies more than
the poetry of Elizabeth Bishop
yet I dig Liz just the same, but
you can eat cookies, poverty wing
nut in the pancake batter, song
fest pushed through a sieve makes
an animated river, doowah diddy
broken car jack is the last place
the police will look when they come
seeping through our abundant tears.
Pick your membrane, death by

firing squad beats carcinogenic
sofa doilies hands down, dawg,
detonate gum drops in lieu of
exaggerated thread count can you
dig how the totals were arrived at?
The number of feathers of a goose
assassinated midair, the dog already
a plunge, is not the dream of orgasms
confettied through a capital storm,
everyone guilty and innocent like
Vegas lights flashing the news that
Elvis has returned and will lead a march
of impersonators, pompadours and sequins,
on the capitol; that is the formula
for turning the screw ever tighter
on the braid of stone and vapor
that binds our love to this fragile place.

Lion, or Cancer?

It's not quite
'strawberry or chocolate' is it?
Mirella, who has been in the African bush,
been chilled by the midnight roar
resounding across the savannah,
can't decide, given the choice,
which she won't be afforded.

Who gets to choose besides the suicide?
What we consider despair is also
a great gesture of freedom,
if anything is free.

How long does it take
for a lion to kill you?
Might depend on motive,
hunger or annoyance?
She might just leave you
maimed and writhing?
You'd think a middle-aged bourgeois victim
would taste like shit:
chock-a-block saturated with poison
and other disgusting modernity.
Lion would have to be mighty peckish
to gag that shit down;
hardly young wildebeest
brought to earth after a vigorous run,

heart still pumping the blood
to the end of every hoof, lip, and kidney.

Cancer, or lion, you won't get that choice,
but if you did? Cancer is boring, a cliché,
happens all the fucking time,
whereas lion, an apex predator,
lion is always violently primary.
She might start eating you before you were dead.
Imagine that. First she'd rip out your inner organs,
stomach, liver, that's how they get their greens.
The pain would probably fry your brain before
your heart gave it up or you bled out.

Carcinogen or King of the Jungle?
Sounds like an ancient Roman game show
only their medicine wasn't that precise
and neither is ours.
While we relentlessly give ourselves cancer
in an ever expanding variety of ways,
we've not given alternative deaths much thought.
As science grows ever more accurate in predicting
our coming inevitable demises, there should be
a market for choosing something visceral and primal.
FOOD FOR WORMS, OR FOOD FOR LION?
THINK ABOUT IT.

So Much Depends Upon Celery

Not red wheelbarrows or chickens,
love and the smeared residue of
but celery, seleeno, as they say here
and we use it everywhere that needs
a touch of bitterness and really,
what doesn't? We don't seek a balance
as much as a vibrant mix, tastes
colliding with each other and
changing everything with these
collisions. The flavor of the world
is one thing after another: celery,
garlic, fennel, coriander, betrayal
and loss. Relentless the end of things
and so we are vigilant on the flavor,
texture, nose of what we make and
conscious that it only lingers and does
not last, a smack, a relish, a mash
of our fellow living things held in
the mouth like sacrament without faith.

We honor where we live when pretending
to magic the ingredients of the planet come
together in our hands with tastes transcending
our skills or luck but torn into edible proportion
and transformed into all that we are becoming.

It's Not Very Far Away
But It Takes a While To Get There

The crow is no help at all
and don't kid yourself, it's not
about the journey, the getting there.
Life is about being here,
or there, but the in-between?
Nah, it hardly matters.
For instance, I'll soon fly to
Portland, Oregon, a long-dreary-
multiple-stopped-canned-air-
endurance-test: fuck the journey,
it sucks. And anyway, the passage
is a given, even if you're static,
the body is aging away, you don't
even have to think about it.
For instance, today I drive into Sparti
for a bit of shopping. Everything
is closed save for the odd café. Huh?
Epiphany! That's what it is!
The goddamn manifestation of the Christ
as revealed by the visitation of the
wise guys schlepping prezzies. That's right,
you're getting a little history, or mythology
here, even if it's from a blasphemous heathen
such as myself. How neatly ironic that
yours truly, a wise guy all my life,
should forget those clever dudes bearing
gifts. Epiphany, Einstein's first was being

given a compass as a small child and
realizing there was an unseen force at work.
There still is, Al, the curvature of spacetime
doesn't tell me why gravity sucks.
In the, far as we can tell, infinite expanse
of spacetime how would one determine
beginnings and endings? All is flux,
panda rei, as Heraclitus said, and nothing more.
There is no closer, no further, and nothing
in-between. It's getting late early.
At any moment Dominic Sargent will be born.
And that will be something that was not before.

Nobody There

I enjoy posting poetry to the dead
as a shout-out to those a drift
in the void, dog-club afternoon
the flies are a buzzing, the shouts
of children playing drift in, the day
stretches out like a lazy cat and the
shadows of the tree put the wall in play.

But the dead have no head to nod,
no lips to wet, no ponder to mind.
The poems pass through nothing
as though that is what it is.

Crossing Over

Alice writes she's pregnant
and leaves a link to
Go Fuck Me till I qualify
as a community of pilgrims
just glowing with abuse.

Alan reveals that his lips
are full of an electric charge
that give his kisses a
turbo-glow reality.

Upon entering the tholos dome
of Agamemnon's tomb
a boy soprano caressed the air
with a series of notes
that had a pre-birth quality.

A collection was taken for Alice
for whatever she was doing
or going to and I put the forty
in my pocket in, like a fingers
crossed raffle of prize unknown.

There's no passion in compassion
but a letting go of gravity,
it might feel like the ground
is free of you but that's
just the illusion of reward.

They thought everyone's motive
was suspect, more complicated
than a revolution and faster than
fear pealed like a skin. But it was
just one step after another.

A goat on the cliff ledge bleats,
woven through the hairs
a burr on the dog's tail clings,
a black redstart hops in the
trumpet vine, withholding song.

Didn't hear from Alice for months
and then a card posted in Laredo
saying she'd gone to Texas to abort,
defiant, something about sabotage,
crossing over into enemy territory.

We sat around talking about courage,
and why we didn't have much, but
we were glowing with pride for Alice
and the little bit of her victory
we could claim a part of.

Calamity's Child

I think, if I teetered
that way instead, I'd be dead,
that is I'd fall down
the stairs, the earth racing
up to meet me, but it's a
maybe, really, as I've survived
the previous, as everyone
reading this has.
We fall down until
the time we don't
get up.

And the line:
"Hot tramp, I love you so"
is, briefly, stuck in my mind
while turning the compost.
Now there are plenty of reasons
such a delightful bit might
lodge itself in one's consciousness.
The paradox, the derogatory declaration
of love and desire, has a certain
'kiss me, you fool' panache,
of which we are in short supply.
I sing it out.

But really, I'm talking to worm,
tunneling through the steamy mess.

It passes right through and is the
better for it, that is, a handle is turned
and the rotation of solid things
is reversed, and then again.
What is the gender of that
burrowing invertebrate?

We are expanded by tears,
not reduced, and wanting falls out
the window and hits the ground
before wings sprout, let alone feathers.
They are only desire and need,
fleshless invisible forelimbs
that leave the air undisturbed.
O fantasy flapping falling through
decades of misery and resentment!
There's no return from the way out,
there's no turning back, there's nothing
static about static electricity! It's fucking
jumping outta your fingers like a
Star Wars character channeling the force
and zapping the parental unit!
You are the energy conductor!
You are responsible for everything
you've done and will do.

Not Flying But Falling

Someone pushed me outta the plane without a chute,
but fortunately, it's a long way down, and I'm falling
in a most peculiar way. And the stars are blotted by the sun.
I can't see the end from here but I imagine giant neon
block letters spelling: EAT, or END, it doesn't matter.
Why is it only the soon to be executed that get a final meal?
For the rest, a blue plate special at the counter,
sugar dispenser with a saltine cracker in it
and the cool feel of puke green linoleum,
a piece of pecan pie with a big scoop of vanilla.

It is our mothers who push us, knowing it isn't about flying.
Anyone can fall, bend with the gravity of life that heads
in one direction only, air of life whooshing by, like the
illusion of meaning and what arrival portends but often, it feels
a drift, suspended as though rising rather than falling,
but above is just a hollow turbulent rumor.

Simone Weil, still hungry, climbs an abstracted ladder,
testing the weight of air churned by falling,
dense and soft mass pushed and spun by the ineffable,
flattened 'gainst the crush of anticipation,
made a spoor, a tadpole, a sheep pellet on the tongue
which struggles to form words beyond pain
and its antidote. The one given the control group,
the god dream, the placebo decoder ring.
She has a rapport with emptiness

and waves her arms as though they were
feathered appendages and she with the strength
to lift off. The strength to lift off. To turn
descent into glide, soar, float. Buoyant.
But her hairless arms are thin and flail, flap
and plead through the air rushing by.

In the Turning

Tits and sparrows hop and sing
through the bougainvillea.
A chainsaw on a nearby hill whines
through an olive trunk.
Valonian oaks having finally shed
last year's leaves rapidly bud.
At a table in the shade I carve away
at artichokes, spikey and resistant.
They need fistfuls of fennel and dill
topped off with an avgolemono.
Snow on the mountains above
is melting to bare stone.
Everything pretends to be new
though it happens every year.

Something Like Summer Lurks in Laconia

Barren of man the beach stretches north.
Two crows, philosophers, more than likely,
walk the water's edge
considering grains of sand.

Sweetened by a tinge of green
the hard Mani mountains
loom over the bay.

Slow rolling undulation,
a fun house mirror,
naked we stroke and glide
across its murmured surface.

Long pre-breakfast swims
in the late October sea.
What a luxury.

A Tree is Not a Woman

There's a lot of pain ahead,
of that we can be sure.
For every living thing.
And okay, the end,
but what else is certain,
stone cold guaranteed?

*

Try to calibrate consequence.

*

Under the banner of 'Maybe' the struggles of life are waged,
the defeats categorized, a string of moments, a fugue, perhaps,
a melodic construction, water moving down, an epileptic seizure,
a two AM eureka.

*

With these pills will wings sprout?
Will the horizon be sooner than ever?
Will it last?

*

It's a problem, 'cause deep in my heart
I don't really believe
that we shall overcome some day.
And me, what am I overcoming,
privileged swine that I am?
What good does it do,
awareness of privilege,
for any-fucking-body?

*

Forget the hawk's cry that brings the cats' hair up
but remember the air coming down off the mountain
making the trees melancholy sing: around the planet
their brethren are screaming, filling the atmosphere
with the residue of their demise, a bleached solar shriek.
My ear to a olive trunk, 200 years easy, I listen for
something collective. How does the message travel?
There must be sonic persuasions beyond our ken,
frequencies of agony known only to needle and leaf.
How it must pain, Ponderosa to olive and oak,
Conifer to Cyprus, the great roar of a forest on fire?
I press an ear to the rough brittle olive bark, nothing.
I find a tree big enough to hug
but a tree is not a woman,
it is so much more of and slower,
stoic in its encounter with the living;
for what is affection in the botanic world?

*

The Aegean flashes in the afternoon light
and a warm glow suffuses the air. In a post
swim swoon we sprawl on the sand.
Staring out to sea, Mirella says, "I have a request."
"Pray tell?"
"I want 'Gracias a la vida' played at my funeral."
The sea murmurs a curling shuush.
"Okay."
"The Mercedes Sosa version."
"Duly noted."
"Will you remember?"

"I'm writing it down. See? You're good to go."

"The rest, I don't care."

A faintest lick up the sand, the sea.

"Okay, but I don't think I'll be there."

"Why not?"

"I'd say odds are I'm beating you outta here."

"Humpf. We'll see."

A woman is not a tree.

Fuck Death

Too often I find myself
in an elegiac mood.
It's not to be trusted, memory,
but I knew him and often
we laughed, and if we were drunk,
we laughed louder.
Annoyed or envious we drew
the looks of strangers,
some wondered what we took
or how life turned that
laughter would be the result,
that day became night
and day again, the whole mess
of it fanning panoramic out
with nothing to show for it
but a warm vibration left
in our pratfall wake.
We were tripping because
we were watching the birds
rather than our feet.
Hey, we fancied ourselves
slapstick vaudevillians not waiting
but searching for something Beckett.

I have lost track of privilege,
there are so many ways to cut it:
comfort at birth and youth,

metabolism built for pleasure,
the ability to recognize in another
that chair-out-the-window spark,
howl-at-the-moon quirk, flaw in
the weave that frays obedience.
These brothers of mine,
not a one put on a uniform,
picked up a gun to serve
the empire. It wasn't the right
shape for our hands, we couldn't
imagine taking that man's life
before he took ours.

As my youth expired I fled
to a place I didn't belong,
twice outside of comfort zone,
in attendance to the living
and far away...

They go down, my brothers,
young ghosts once with poetry in
their mouths who stumbled into
parenthood and careers,
a prerogative of privilege,
now otherwise engaged with
adventures autoimmune, which
is open to everyone.
I do not regret leaving.
I did not have to watch

their descent or view
the queue at the clinic.
At a distance
I gave my tortured take
on their beliefs and mine.
I tried to make a godless nothing
sound like a lark
a last laugh table slap
a carnival ride into the void.

Some laughed,
some ground their teeth,
others screamed with glee.

All let go for we had closed
the tavern at the end of the world
and there was naught else
but to sing the stars
fading as the dawn came on
and the shadows of the living
swept the ghosts away.

www.ingramcontent.com/pod-product-compliance
Lightning Source LLC
Chambersburg PA
CBHW030532080526
44586CB00011B/405